My Heart Longs To Be Loved

By Tom Gregersen

Tom Gregersen

1-7-13

My Heart Longs To Be Loved

My Heart Longs To Be Loved©

2012
Tom Gregersen
Eugene, OR USA

ISBN-13:978-1479306756

ISBN-10:1479306754

Holy Bible verses are taken from the New International Version, NIV©, 1973, 1978, 1984, 2011 by Biblica, Inc. All rights reserved.

Publishing: Audacious Consulting©, Eugene, OR. www.annettetrucke.com

Table of Contents

Forward

My Heart Longs To Be Loved penned by Tom Gregersen, is a collection of poems that resonate with the heart. For those of you who have the honor of knowing Tom, you will automatically "get" his poems. He is a man of great heart and a ready sense of humor which is easily identified by his good-natured smirk and the glimmer shown in his eyes. His boyish humor will entertain you and his pearls of wisdom will be sure to connect your heart to your brain.

Tom is a giver. Therefore I suggest that you take his words as a gift to you, the reader, as he extends sparks of joy, knowing compassion, and God-breathed hope to all who read his verbiage given cadence.

Annette Trucke
Audacious Consulting
Eugene, OR

My Heart Longs To Be Loved

Endorsements

"There truly is no one else like Tom. He is a witty, caring, kind and giving man of God. Tom's poems always come from his heart. Whether they are silly or moving, they tell a story that needs to be heard. He is someone who will both laugh and cry with you, and his writings reflect his compassion."

"I have the privilege of calling him my friend."

Julie Davis/Friend
Eugene, OR

"Within these pages Tom Gregersen invites you to explore and enjoy the depths of his heart and the laughter of his soul."

Jacque Langenberg/Guidance Counselor
Eugene, OR

"I have had the privilege of knowing "Rec Tom" for almost three decades and have learned so much from his life, his love, his kindness and his compassion. Someone said that people are impressed at a distance, but impacted up close. He has impacted so many by his tender heart for God and his caring heart for people. We can be confident that out of the overflow of the heart, the mouth speaks... and the pen writes. You will be blessed by the overflow of Tom's heart."

"Finally, since this is a creative compilation of some of Tom's insights and wisdom, I thought I would summarize my thoughts in a poem dedicated to the author..."

*"Roses are red, violets are blue,
Tommy G is a very fine fellow with a deeply compassionate spirit
And is a much better poet than I am."*

Dave (the Wave) Mertz,
Eugene, OR

~ONE~

My Heart Longs To Be Loved

My heart longs to be loved
Said the sexually abused teenager,
Not the kind that rips and tears
But the kind that builds trust and repairs.

My heart longs to be loved,
Said the unnerved foster child.
Kids shouldn't be throw aways,
And families should be main stays.

My heart longs to be loved
Says the physically abused wife,
More than my throat was damaged,
When he tried to strangle me twice.

My heart longs to be loved,

Says the old man confined to a

Nursing home.

Why have friends and family forgotten

That I am warehoused and all alone?

~TWO~

Proverbs 15:13 A happy heart makes the face cheerful, but heartache crushes the spirit.

Banish the Frown

You're never too young.

You're never too old.

To stretch for dreams,

Be daring and bold.

Why sit on a shelf and mold?

Or get on your high horse and scold?

Sail around the world; build a life.

Rebound from the death of your wife.

Wake up with a smile.

Banish the frown.

Include the Spirit's covering

As you slip into your gown.

For we weren't meant to stumble

On earth all alone.

We need to seek direction,

But not from an I-Phone.

~THREE~

A mom is a precious gift, and mom's that take on foster kids and orphans face huge challenges and can be an amazing treasure from God. Anita Gregersen was that person for me caring for me from age seven to 15 and finally able to adopt me. 1 Thessalonians 2:7 says "we were gentle among you like a mother caring for her little children." There is strength in gentleness that quiets and heals a wounded heart. This poem is dedicated to the woman who was that fountain of healing for me.

Anita

Anita was barely five feet tall,

A giant in heart,

In stature so small,

Authorities branded her too old

To mother a child, so she was told.

Rules and guidelines agencies make,

Can't define the real mom from the fake.

Real moms create from a heart of love,

Sent by their Creator from high above.

Real moms believe in the best everyday,

They never give up, no matter

What people say,

"That child is damaged, he's really

No good,

He'll break your heart,

At least he should."

Small in stature,

A giant in heart,

She changed the life of one torn apart.

A mom's love can do that, it did for me.

Some call it chance,

I call it destiny.

~FOUR~

Humpty Dumpty was written when I lay in a hospital bed for over a week with pneumonia. You might say I wrote it in a delirious state, because I had very high temperatures, but I wrote it because I was bored and my weird sense of humor has helped me face many different seasons of life. Ecclesiastes 3:1 says, "There is a time for everything, and a season for every activity under the sun."

Humpty Dumpty is dedicated to all of my grandchildren.

Humpty Dumpty

(Verse)

Humpty Dumpty lay in the

Emergency ward,

Staring at the ceiling,

He was completely bored.

And as he lay there,

He was heard to say,

That was a no, no,

I pulled the other day.

(Chorus)

No, no, no, no,

Won't do it again.

No, no, no, no,

You never can win.

No, no, no, no,

Won't do it no more,

Cause it's hard for an egg

To get up off the floor.

(Verse)

Humpty Dumpty lay stretched

Out in his bed,

Cracked from his naval,

Right up to his head.

And all the kings horses,

And all the kings men,

Couldn't get Humpty on top

Of that wall again.

(Chorus)

No, no, no, no,

Won't do it again.

No, no, no, no,

You never can win.

No, no, no, no,

Won't do it no more,

Cause it's hard for an egg

To get up off the floor.

(Verse)

Chicken, chicken,

They would yell at him.

You hard boiled fools,

I am no hen.

And so one day,

Just to prove them wrong

He decided to jump,

Taking a parachute along.

(Chorus)

No, no, no, no,

Won't do it again.

No, no, no, no,

You never can win.

No, no, no, no,

Won't do it no more,

Cause it's hard for an egg

To get up off the floor.

(Verse)

Shell I do it---yes I must

And I don't care even if I bust my yoke,

Cause an egg has to have pride,

Or He'll end up broken and fried.

~FIVE~

I am always fascinated by the fact that we are to work together as Christians like a body must work to be healthy. I Corinthians 12 makes it quite clear that there should be no division in the body of Christ. My fascination comes from how unwilling we are to cooperate and how quickly we sow seeds of discontent and divide.

Body Mutiny!

If the hand said to the ear,

I am going to spank you my dear.

If the finger said to the eye,

I'll poke you, by and by.

If the tongue said to the lips,

I'd rather hang around the hips.

If the belly button got unzipped,
Stuff would spill out until we tripped.

If the fingernail refused to scratch,
That itchy, prickly infested patch
Of poison oak on one's back,
A good night's sleep we'd lack.

If my shoulder refused to raise my arm,
When my brain signaled there
Was an alarm.
It would be hard to get out of bed
If my leg were an eyebrow instead.

We should work in harmony everyday
As our body works in a normal way.
Otherwise, you better watch out,
A train is coming,
And your kneecap can't shout!

~SIX~

The Bible is full of people who were given a second chance by the Lord. If you ever feel like giving up on yourself, remember that God doesn't give up on you. He will never leave, forsake or give up on you!

Second Chances

Everyone needs a second chance,

To learn to live to love and dance,

We all take missteps and lose our way,

So thanks Jesus, for the patience

Offered today.

Sometimes we are prone to give up,

But our Savior offers a clean cup.

A chance to follow where He leads,

While he supplies daily needs.

Everyone needs to believe

They can change,

That they can alter direction

Or rearrange.

Decisions and habits that need altering

So that they can carry on

Without faltering.

Everyone needs someone

Who believes the best

In each of us that will stand the test.

Of times, and trials, and ups-and-downs

And exchange our scars for golden crowns.

~SEVEN~

I remember a time I came in very exhausted from a day of yard work, and my mother-in-law started berating me for not helping my wife. I reacted in anger. Now that I look back on it, I wish that I had known some of the underlying problems she had that I didn't find out about until after her death. Had I known I might have reacted differently, but it doesn't change the fact that I could have responded with a soft answer and avoided hurt feelings for both of us.

A Soft Answer

A soft answer turns away wrath,

A Bible truth that most of us know.

So why is it so easy to explode?

And, so hard our temper to control?

A soft answer calms storms,

Before they escalate into raging fires

That damage relationships permanently,

Leaving charred remains

And crossed wires.

A soft answer turns the tide

Of churning emotions,

Like raging oceans

That need room to subside.

A soft answer is like a cool breeze,

On a hot and humid day.

Sent from heaven, spreading relief,

For all who travel along life's way.

~EIGHT~

We all face the challenge of materialism and wanting more than we really need. The Bible talks about the eye of man never being satisfied, and that is particularly true of the eye of women—if they get near an outlet mall. Ecclesiastes 5:13-14a states that there is a grievous evil, under the sun; wealth hoarded to the harm of its owner.

Hoarding

It all started with collecting lamps,

Unlike others who start with stamps.

There are desk lamps and hanging ones,

Ones who weigh ounces and

Those who weigh tons.

Clothes are really very easy to collect,

You can't have enough ties

To decorate the neck.

Blouses, dresses and skirts,
Pants, undies, shorts and shirts.

Blue and yellow, brown and red,
Checkered and striped from toe to head.
Pull-on and pull-overs, pleated and prints,
Bright colors, neutral colors,
Solids and tints.

Tin cans, cookie jars, fish tanks
And books,
Stuff in drawers, shelves, crannies
And nooks.
Pocket watches, coins, silverware
And trash,
You can collect anything if you spend
Enough cash.

Hoarding is fun and soon you are hooked,
There's hardly anything you've overlooked.

You can't get in your house,

Or lay on your bed,

Cause you need to fill

The place with treasures instead.

~NINE~

Proverbs 31 does a wonderful job defining what a Godly, spiritual woman is like. Proverb 31 women have a tremendous impact on their children and husbands and they are to be appreciated and honored. I have been fortunate enough to have a mother, two wives and a daughter that demonstrate the qualities that are described in this portion of Scripture. I love the verse that states that "charm is deceptive, and beauty is fleeting; but a woman who fears the Lord is to be praised."

Four Proverb 31 Ladies

Anita was drawn

With determination and grit,

A human dynamo

Who was not intimidated a bit.

She desired to be a mom

More than diamonds or fame.

And she helped an abandoned boy

Realize he had a name.

Joanne was beauty drawn with grace,

She had a smile that lit up her face.

She breathed love in my life

That was lasting and true,

My sweetheart brought hope

And stability into view.

Tanya is drawn like a beautiful gazelle,

Sensitive and charming, sketched so well.

She loves children and possesses

A special gift,

To nurture and cause their

Spirits to lift.

Becky is drawn with strokes broad

And true,

Strong and bold with wisdom too.

Kind and encouraging she brings a smile,

That has made my days happy and

Worthwhile.

~TEN~

I wrote this song/poem for a 6th grade girl named Amy who was crushed by her parents divorce. During a retreat she lit a candle and proclaimed her flame was faltering but wouldn't go out.

1 Corinthians 13:7 tells us that: Love always perseveres, or never gives up!

A Small Flame

I hold a small flame somewhere within,

Barely flickering, fragile and dim.

I hold a small flame, sometime without,

And although it falters with fear and doubt,

It won't go out, It won't go out!

(Chorus)

Some call the flame love,

Some call the flame desire,

If there was enough Love,
It would ignite into fire.

Somehow the flame I have may
Guide another.
Someday the light I share may
Help a brother.
I hold a small flame and regardless
Of your name
My flame can reach you if you
Have a flame too.

(Chorus)
Some call the flame love,
Some call the flame desire,
If there was enough Love,
It would ignite into fire.

Fire to destroy indifference
And to swallow up lies,

To burn down barriers

And selfish cries.

Wiping out jealousy and defeating hate,

No more bad examples to imitate.

(Chorus)

Some call the flame love,

Some call the flame desire,

If there was enough Love,

It would ignite into fire.

I hold a small flame somewhere within.

I hold a small flame shaky and dim.

Just enough light with which to begin,

There'll be more light if you'll join in.

My Heart Longs To Be Loved

~ELEVEN~

It is easy for us to preach contentment and hard to live it. The times we aren't content we are basically forgetting or denying that God is in control. I Timothy 6:6 reminds us, "that godliness with contentment is great gain."

Contentment

I was driving one day

When a Chevy cut me off.

My reaction was inappropriate

From a man of the cloth.

I had some advice

That I wanted to share,

Then I wanted to rip the driver

Out by his hair.

My wife was trying to give me

A helpful recommendation,

On how to keep our house

From condemnation.

She suggested that I actually

Could pick up after myself,

And it would be helpful

To return the books to the shelf.

I willingly listen to hear her say

That I should clean up my act

Starting today.

I pretend to listen

With an open mind,

And then leave her counsel

Far behind.

I am happy and content

Both day and night.

I never worry,

Fuss or fight.

And if you were ever to see
Me protest,
It's a shame you didn't catch
Me at my best.

~TWELVE~

This poem was prompted by a member of my extended family who talks at record speed. Proverbs 20:19 states, "A gossip betrays a confidence; so avoid a man who talks too much."

Fast Talking

Did you know, did you hear?

That if you let me, I'll talk off your ear.

I have lots and lots to say,

About all that happened yesterday.

And all that will happen tomorrow,

And all the gossip I can borrow.

Did you hear? Do you know?

That the Mayor broke his toe?

And have you heard that's not all
That happened when he took the fall?
What? What's that you say?
You have inside information on Elly May?

Who she was with, and what she did,
Oh if you tell me, I'll keep it under my lid.
Have you heard my latest story
About yesteryear's fame and glory?

I can bore you until the cows come in,
And then take a breath and start again.
Maybe if I could turn down the flow,
I could listen, learn and grow.
But then how could I tell you, all the
Billion, trillion things I know?

~THIRTEEN~

This is a poem I wrote a year ago and as I am at this time a week away from my 70th birthday it seems like a good poem to consider.

Finish Strong

I want to finish strong,

Like the melody to a song,

That lingers in your brain,

A compelling refrain.

I want to finish strong,

Whether my race is short or long.

I want to run hard with heart,

I want to finish what I start.

I want to run with Jesus Christ,

Because you get to run once, not twice.

I want to follow his lead,
And run with purpose and speed.

I want to train with the best,
And heed His advice and past the test.
I want to show up on the day of the race,
Run with endurance and push the pace.

Until some day when the race is over,
I will rest in a patch of heaven's clover,
And hear my master say
With His eternal word,
Well done while on earth, because
My voice you heard.

~FOURTEEN~

His Eye is on the Sparrow
Matthew 10:29

He cares for us when we are lonely,
Watches over us when we are lost.
He guides and directs each life,
No matter what the cost.

We may run away from Him,
Try things that aren't the best,
But He never abandons us,
He offers peace and rest.

He knows when we're afraid,
When we dash and dart about.
When walls crash down on us,
He hears our muffled cry
And desperate shout.

He wipes away the tears,

That cascade down our face.

He holds us up close and comforts us,

With His comforting embrace.

His eye is on the sparrow,

He sees their impending fall.

His heart is for his children,

He hears their every call.

~FIFTEEN~

All of us would like to be in charge and have things go our way. Even the greatest kings in the Bible found that "being King" didn't solve all their problems.

King for a Day

If I could be king for a day,

Everyone would be interested

In what I say.

I would order people

To do my chores, and bow to me

As I entered doors.

Everyone would want my autograph,

And if I gave them a smile,

They would be happy and proud, for my

Smile would make their year worthwhile.

If I were king, I would

Order buckets of ice cream.

And if I sang a song,

It would make all the girl's scream.

While I was king I would wear golden PJ's.

And if I wrote rap songs,

They would be played by famous D.J.'s

But fame is fleeting

And so are good looks.

And even if I were talented and

Wrote books,

I wouldn't be as happy,

I wouldn't be as smart,

As if I were wise enough to honor

The real King in my heart!

51

~SIXTEEN~

The Lazy Ant

There was an ant so lazy,

That he drove the others crazy.

He boycotted picnics and most food.

The other ants thought him extremely

Rude.

He wouldn't do his share,

And this was obviously unfair,

To brothers, a million or more,

Who gathered supplies in the store.

He would sit and stare,

While he rocked in his chair.

Or played video games all day,

While others gathered hay.

Life is short, have some fun!

Sit and relax in the warm sun.

But none of his buddies or next of kin,

Would agree to go along with him.

So one day when he was getting a tan,

The others decided to lend him a hand.

They exiled him to an island far away,

And he hasn't been seen since that day.

~SEVENTEEN~

Class reunions help us evaluate our lives and the ultimate reunion we will have with our Creator. We all hope He will say, "Well done, good and faithful servant." Will we be able to assert like Paul that we have kept the faith and been obedient to our Master?

Memory Lane

"I have fought the good fight, I have finished the race, I have kept the faith."

II Timothy 4:7

This weekend I took a stroll
Down memory lane.
Fifty year reunions leave
Very little the same.

We were 18 years young
And devising future schemes,
Clutching a diploma
Full of hopes and dreams.
Our most promising graduate,
That was destined for glory
Took his own life,
A sobering and tragic story.

Others continued to live in the past,
Because their glory days were such a blast.
Some who were not expected
To prosper and shine,
Present quite a legacy as they left
High school behind.

So when you work with young people,
And you think you know
How they'll turn out,
Give them room to grow.

~EIGHTEEN~

My wife of forty years, Joanne, was diagnosed with leukemia and died 8 months later. During her care in a Seattle hospital she talked of a nurse that worked on the graveyard crew that took incredibly good care of her. She was impressed with the kindness and care of the nurse with red hair and button-blue eyes. This poem is dedicated to all the nurses that really show the compassion that the Lord desires from each one of us. (Luke 10:36-37)

Button-blue Eyes

Red hair and button blue eyes,

That's how my wife described her.

With a smile on her face,

She described this lady of grace.

Her nurse for the night,

An angel in white,

I wish you could know,

How you blessed her so.

She lost her fight for life,

My brave courageous wife.

But you were a beacon

In the midst of a storm.

You were the blanket,

So soft and warm.

Red hair and button-blue eyes,

How I wish you could realize,

The difference a nurse

Who cares can make.

The comfort you gave

For love's pure sake.

~NINETEEN~

Many of us struggle with anger and the lack of ability to control our temper. Proverbs 16:32 states that, "better is a patient man than a warrior, a man who controls his temper than one who takes a city."

Temper Tantrum

One day I decided to blow my top,

Fizzy steam spilled over like bottled pop.

Lava spilled over my face and eyes,

While clouds of anger continued to rise.

I told everyone that I had had it,

And proceeded to throw a world record fit.

I fell to the floor and kicked my feet,

In a temper tantrum that was hard to beat.

When things calmed down,
And the air was clear,
People crept out of hiding,
Like startled deer.
They waited to see
If after-shocks were looming,
So they could clear out if
Explosions were resuming.

When we blow our tops
We leave gaping holes,
Debris from our outbursts
Trouble other souls.
When we lose control
We lose more than we realize,
We lose the trust in relationships
Which slowly dies.

~TWENTY~

For seven years I worked at a Christian camp located at an elevation where the stars put on a light show each night, reminding me of truth of Psalms 19:1-2— "The heavens declare the glory of God the skies proclaim the work of his hands."

Twinkle, Twinkle

Twinkle, twinkle stars so bright,

A million, billion shine in the night,

Proclaiming the glory of the creator,

In the canopy of darkness, His theater.

How can one view the galaxies,

And not realize the great fallacies

Of denying creation's majestic show

And saying the Creator is not so?

We cloud creation with earthly worries,

Viewing God's greatness

In occasional flurries.

Dimmed by our rush to gather and rule,

We play the part of the self-absorbed fool.

God's handiwork is on display most nights,

His heaven is full of luminous insights,

Proclaiming His creativity

And infinite might,

Hosting unrivaled brilliance

Of starry light.

~TWENTY-ONE~

Unless the Lord

Unless the Lord builds the camp,

The fundraising projects are in vain.

Unless the Lord watches over the camp,

The campers will drive you insane.

Unless the Lord builds the school,

Students will ignore the golden rule.

Knowledge may be taught,

But wisdom ignored,

Honor goes to men,

Not to our holy Lord.

Unless the Lord builds the marriage,

Division and selfishness may creep in.

Partners will consider personal happiness

More important than the vows made to
Him.

Unless the Lord builds the family,
Dysfunction may rule the day.
Because each member will be prone
To seek and demand their own way.

~TWENTY-TWO~

Weeds are like sin. It doesn't take much to grow them, but it takes a lot of effort to get rid of them. Hebrews 12:1 talks about sin that so easily entangles; a lot like weeds.

Weeds

There was a woman that pulled weeds

That didn't even belong to her.

She pulled them wherever

They sprouted to life,

They didn't stand a chance for sure.

Wouldn't it be great if we all pulled weeds

Wherever and whenever they dared to

Show?

It wouldn't take an invitation to attack

Much like an army that delivered a blow.

Weeds grow silently and quickly,

They form in all of our daily lives.

They can be loud like fights and spats,

Or quiet like jealously and lies.

Most of us tend to wait too late

To rid ourselves of weeds that we sow.

We have to be diligent and quick to assail,

Because weeds take little effort to grow.

Made in the USA
Charleston, SC
14 December 2012